Armorbearer
A LIFE OF SERVICE

Armorbearer
A LIFE OF SERVICE

The Master Key to
Greatness and Significance

Tolu Areola

Cover credit: Beautiful Idea Graphics
beautifulideagraphics@gmail.com

ISBN-13: 978-0-9968340-0-1
ISBN-10: 0996834001
Library of Congress Control Number: 2015916240

Published by Empowerment For Today
Made in USA 2015
Email: contact@empowermentfortoday.com
www.empowermentfortoday.com

Printed in the United States of America

To

My Friend, HOLY SPIRIT

Thank You

Dedication

Lovingly dedicated to the love of my life, Jesus Christ, whose love is unfailing and whose blessing is beyond measure.

He placed two people in my life who have impacted me eternally, Pastors Toye and Wumi Ademola.
They provide a spiritual covering and care as pastors, teachers, mentors, and parents in the Lord.

Their tutelage, Christ-like examples, and faithful prayers have made all the difference in God's divine placement and agenda for my life.

For this, I am forever grateful.

Acknowledgments

My heartfelt thanks go to my parents, Professor Olusegun and Dr. (Mrs.) Esther Areola, the ones who first taught me, through their great model, that to lead is to serve.

A very big thank you to these precious friends who challenge me to stand out and not blend in. You are golden links to destiny and incredible additions to my life: Seye Omole, Gbemi and Kemi Olawale, Kola and Nike Olaleye, Tunde and Seun Akeredolu, Kunle and Bola Akindele, Phillip and Grace Ayodele, Bisola Oviawe, Barbara Fandrich, and the staff and members of Dominion International Center.

I am indebted to all my mentors whose teachings and inspiration have helped my learning and application of the truths I have shared in this book.

My sincere gratitude to my sunshine, Tomi, and our children, Joy and Joshua. Your support, encouragement, and prayers sustain me, and are a blessing to me. Thank you for a home without thorns.

Contents

FOREWORD
13

INTRODUCTION
15

UNDERSTANDING ARMORBEARING   CHAPTER ONE
The Master Key Code   23

ARMORBEARING 101   CHAPTER TWO
Developing the Spirit of an Armorbearer   39

ARMORBEARING 102   CHAPTER THREE
Developing the Soul of an Armorbearer   65

ARMORBEARING 103   CHAPTER FOUR
The Process of Transformation   73

ARMORBEARING 104   CHAPTER FIVE
Four Kinds of Servants   89

ARMORBEARING 105   CHAPTER SIX
The Rewards of Armorbearing   97

ARMORBEARING 106   CHAPTER SEVEN
The Leadership of Servanthood   109

ARMORBEARING 107   CHAPTER EIGHT
The Grace to Serve   121

On a Personal Note   137
About the Author   139
Appendix and Notes   140

FOREWORD

If there were ever a man qualified to write a book on kingdom service and significance, Tolu Areola is the man!

For two decades, I have personally witnessed and been greatly blessed by his consistent, diligent, and excellent service to God at our church and ministry. Literally, right from the moment Tolu surrendered his heart to the Lord Jesus Christ in 1996, he hit the ground running! Like the Energizer Bunny, he has just kept going and going; working for the Lord and with the Lord, nonstop. Through the years, he's served faithfully in several capacities, ranging from being a sound technician to his current position as one of our associate pastors and the director of ministry operations.

Indeed, the time-proven principles that Tolu shares in **Armorbearer, a Life of Service:** *The Master Key to Greatness and Significance* are not the mere words of a man who is just talking the talk. No! They are real wisdom keys based on the actual life experiences of a true servant-leader who has been walking the walk for close to twenty years and counting!

In these end times, servant leaders are the kind of people that God is looking for to help propagate the Gospel and advance His kingdom in the earth. He needs an army of **Armorbearer Christians** who are up and about **the Father's business**; not a bunch of **armchair Christians** who are just concerned about how they can get **the Father's blessings**!

This book is a clarion call to you, my friend, to embrace your destiny as a co-laborer with Jesus in the Father's business *(Luke 2:49)*. Read it meticulously—*from the beginning till the very end*—I guarantee you will not remain the same! You will be gloriously empowered to become the kind of Christian that God has ordained you to be—one who *seeks to serve*, rather than *seeking to be served (Mark 10:43–45)*—**an armorbearer who impacts humanity for God's glory!**

Toye Ademola
September 2015

INTRODUCTION

*"And I will give you the keys of the kingdom of heaven,
and whatever you bind on earth will be bound in heaven,
and whatever you loose on earth will be loosed in heaven"* [1]

We live in an information age where you need key codes to access everything. We need access key codes to get our money out of the ATM machine, to operate our computers and, smart electronic devices, and to gain access into our social media network. Some of us even need access key codes to get into our cars, homes, and work places. Simply put, we live in a world that operates by keys.

As a believer in Jesus Christ, you must understand that you belong to a kingdom system that operates by keys, and with these keys you open whatever doors you desire.

Jesus said "I will give you the keys of the kingdom of heaven, and whatever you bind on earth will be bound in heaven, and whatever you loose on earth will be loosed in heaven."[2]

He was simply saying that His plan for you is to have complete and free access to the best of God's kingdom system, but you can only have this access with the keys He has already made available.

There are keys to having a long and fulfilled life, great health and healing, joy and happiness, peace and prosperity, wealth and riches, overflowing favor, and all-round success. If you lack any of these wonderful blessings of God, it is an indication that you are yet to discover the keys you need to gain access to them.

There are keys that open certain individual doors, but a master key opens ALL doors! This concept of the master key became a revelation to me a few years ago when observing the unbalanced life of some believers. It was disturbing to see believers struggling and stagnant, barely surviving because they did not have what they needed to make it in life. They were trying their hands in so many different things in the pursuit of the good life.

Sons and daughters of a rich God were living in poverty and running the rat race of life. Even though some seemed to be winning the race, the truth remained that they were still rats! Men and women were confessing their redemption and freedom in Christ but still living in the bondage of the enemy, which proved that the problem was not with God but with His people.

God said "My people have gone into captivity, because they have no knowledge; their honorable men are famished, and their multitude dried up with thirst."[3] They did not have the right keys to access the things God had already made available to them because they lacked the knowledge and understanding of the truth. You remain a victim of the lies of the devil if you do not know the truth about what you are going through, and about God's blessings that are available to you by inheritance. John 8:32 says, *"And you shall know the truth, and the truth shall make you free."*

Your knowledge of the truth makes you free to live the best life that God designed for you; the secret is to use the keys He has already made available.

Being stranded and stagnant is the result of not possessing a key or the right key to open a door. However, with the master key, you enjoy all-access and freedom to go as you please. You gain unlimited and unrestricted access regardless of the type of door standing at every entry point. Think of it, just one single key grants you access to all the crucial entryways you need to go through. This is the power of the master key!

In this book, *Armorbearer, a Life of Service,* I present to you the master key to living a fulfilled life and walking the path of success, greatness, and significance as designed by God. Armorbearing is the master key to a fulfilled life. It is the secret to greatness and significance.

In this book, you will learn the true meaning of greatness, and the pathway of real significance in life. The teachings include understanding armorbearing, developing the spirit and soul of an armorbearer, the process of transformation, the four kinds of servants, the rewards of armorbearing, the leadership of Servanthood and the grace to serve. This is an uncommon book that will launch you into an uncommon life of greatness and significance!

For you to achieve what you have never achieved before, you must do what you have never done. But in order to do that, you must change. This book will challenge you to change, to become someone you have never been so you can achieve the success and greatness you desire. There are many principles and teachings on *"what to do"*, but very few on *"whom to become"*. This book will teach you how to become the person God designed for you to be, so what you do will have great and eternal value.

There is no better example to follow than Jesus Christ. Many great men came before Him, but none of them ever made a lasting mark as He did. Men like Theudas and Judas of Galilee[4] came not with a mission of armorbearing but of self-promotion and selfish ambition. Jesus surpassed their impact and results because of the spirit and mission of armorbearing.

He was successful and God gave Him the highest possible place *of glory and significance,* and honored His name above all others.[5]

God has the same plan for you. The seeds of greatness and significance were put in you when the One True Great God created you. He made you in His image and likeness to be the reflection of His glory and greatness because as He is, so are we in this world.[6]

There is a leader trapped in you! There is greatness and significance imprisoned and buried within you! Armorbearing is the access key to the force of freedom that will begin the revealing process; that is the purpose of this book!

The great news is that the rich wisdom, understanding, and knowledge you will gain in this book, when applied, will help you to effect the change you need to enjoy the good life that you have always desired. This book is for people who have the will and intent to change, grow, improve, and achieve their God designed purpose in life.

The focus of today's culture and society is on the search for personal happiness, comfort, peace, success, prosperity, and riches. Many are wildly in search of the right key codes to unlock these different doors of life. Unfortunately, their quest to gain access through the various doors has been futile because they are using the wrong key codes. As a result, they have wasted so much time, energy, and resources.

The right key code gives you access through the right door but only the master key code opens ALL doors! With the master key code, you can unlock any door at will and gain access to the benefits that are loaded behind the doors. This book will show you this master key.

You are about to embark on a life changing journey of discovery and encounter with the potent principles from the word of God. Be blessed!

Tolu Areola
Houston, Texas

Chapter One
UNDERSTANDING ARMORBEARING:
The Master Key Code

"I will bless you with a future filled with hope—
a future of success, not of suffering."[1]

Before defining armorbearing and the importance of this incredible key, it is quite critical to let you know that God's plan for you is a good plan. He promised to bless you with a future filled with hope, a future of success, not of *unnecessary* suffering.[2]

It is a plan of success to bring you prosperity and not disaster, to take care of you and not to abandon you, until you have and enjoy life to the fullest. This is God's plan for you.

Now, it is one thing to know the plan, yet another thing to walk in it. You can see the Promised Land, yet it is another thing to enter it. It is one thing to have insight into the principles of God, yet another thing for you to know them by experience.

These simple but profound statements highlight the true reason success, prosperity, happiness and fulfillment in life have eluded so many people today. Many are chasing the wind; they work hard but have nothing to show for their efforts. They wish and wail for the good life but are not able to enter into it because they have no access. Nevertheless, you can have the access and you can live the good life!

As a Christian, you have a right to this good life because Jesus came to give us that right when He came in human flesh, died on the cross, and was resurrected.[3] By embracing this reality, you have the right and access to a triumphant life! This is the foundation of armorbearing, which is the master key that unlocks every door to a glorious life, and the master key code to success, greatness, and significance! With it, you can access all the dimensions of success in God's system, spiritual, financial, and health—and you can live the triumphant life as planned for you by God.

ARMORBEARING DEFINED

Armorbearing is the divine lifestyle of laying down one's life for another in true service and total commitment. Armorbearing simply means servanthood. It is the art of working in the service of another.[4] The person that lives like this is an armorbearer.

Originally translated from two Hebrew words, **nasa** *(naw-saw')* and **keliy'** *(kel-ee')*, "armorbearer" is a compound word with a truly deep meaning.

The first Hebrew word, *nasa*, means to lift, to bear up, to ease, to extol, to help or to hold up;[5] while *keliy'* means something prepared, an apparatus (such as an implement, utensil, dress, vessel, or weapon).[6]

From these definitions, we can say that an armorbearer is a vessel prepared to bear up or help in service and support. An armorbearer is someone who attends to, ministers to, assists and supports, cares for, or helps and serves another.

"Let's go across to the outpost of those pagans," Jonathan said to his armorbearer. "Perhaps the Lord will help us, for nothing can hinder the Lord. He can win a battle whether he has many warriors or only a few!" "Do what you think is best," the armorbearer replied. "I'm with you completely, whatever you decide."[7]

In biblical days, an armorbearer was someone who acted as a personal assistant to his leader, and was in the service of another regardless of position or status. In the kingdom of God today, we term an armorbearer as a Christian with the spirit of kingdom service, living the life of a servant in the power of the Holy Spirit according to the example of Jesus Christ.

Armorbearing is the Spirit of Jesus Christ. He said of Himself, "The Lord has put His Spirit in Me, because He appointed Me to tell the Good News to the poor. He has sent Me to tell the captives they are free and to tell the blind that they can see again. God sent Me to free those who have been treated unfairly and to announce the time when the Lord will show His kindness."[8]

ARMORBEARER IS WHO YOU ARE

God's plan for you is to be His armorbearer here on earth and to prove that Jesus came to model this lifestyle to us. He is the greatest armorbearer that ever lived. "For even the Son of Man did not come to be served, but to serve and to give His life a ransom for many."[9]

Jesus said to His disciples, "I am among you as the One who serves!"[10] "Yes, I am your Master, Leader, and Lord, yet I have been with you as a servant. This is who I am and you must be the same!"

A lifestyle of service is the single most important key to accessing the great future you desire. Everyone wants to be successful. Everyone wants to be great. Everyone wants to be significant. These desires are manifestations of the "God nature" put in us by the Great Creator Himself. He created you in His image and likeness, with the seeds of greatness implanted within you; and the pathway to see the fruit of your desires is to embrace a life of service.

God's plan for you is to be a contributor to the advancement of humanity, not to be another consumer whose goal is to keep on taking, without giving anything back. God wants you to live a life of success and great achievement but to accomplish that you must become the person He made you to be. You must embrace your identity of armorbearer just as Jesus did. He became our ultimate example of this life so we can live just as He lived here in the world.[11]

Since the fall of man in the Garden of Eden, his outlook and disposition toward life and humanity have been marred by extreme prejudice, self-centeredness, and selfishness. As a result, the whole world began to deteriorate into a place where self-preservation and self-aggrandizement became the norm; therefore the social and economic climate plunged into the decay of tyranny. This was never God's intention when He said, "Let Us make Man in Our image, according to Our likeness."[12] His plan was for us to live just like Him, that is why He calls us gods and children of The Most High.[13] He designed us to reflect His nature and take responsibility for the care and nurture of the earth. This great plan and desire of God has not changed. He created you to be a solution to your world through a lifestyle of service! God designed you to make a difference with the life He gave you, to serve your world.

SERVICE DEFINED

"To serve" means to help, to be of use, to render assistance, or to attend to the needs of someone. It is using your natural and divine endowment in service to humanity and in promoting the kingdom of God on the earth! This is the essence of armorbearing, and it is who you are designed to become. God's desire has always been for man to embrace his true identity as armorbearer; from the days of Abraham, Moses, and Jesus until now, the cry from God for mankind to "serve Him" has not ceased![14]

The Bible says that you are fearfully and wonderfully made,[15] and what God said to Jeremiah is true for you also. He said, "Before I made you in your mother's womb, I chose you. Before you were born, I set you apart for a special work.[16] God constructed you as a biological machine with intricate and delicate parts, with each piece of your equipment designed to perform specific functions toward the encompassing purpose of solving problems. You are not a biological accident! God placed you on this earth for a very special assignment. You are unique in design with your uniqueness geared toward being the answer to the challenging questions of life, spreading the fragrance of God on the earth.

BECOME WHO YOU ARE

As a Christian, your life is not your own because you were bought with a great price; therefore you belong to Jesus Christ.[17] You have no rights of your own to do as you please but rather you must do as commanded by Him so you can become God's armorbearer.

God has made us what we are. In Christ Jesus, God made us to do good works, which God planned in advance for us to live our lives doing.[18] Once you accept this truth, you are free from the burden of carrying the fears and concerns that trouble the people of the world. You will live perpetually under the personal care of God.

DAVID

David was a young man who prior to his trip to Saul's

palace was out in the fields keeping and tending his father's sheep. Back in those days, this job was primarily the work of house servants, however, though a son, David got the "honor" of this task. He embraced the role wholeheartedly, and that forged the foundation of his essence as armorbearer.

Out in the field all alone with the sheep, he would meditate on the wonders of the heavens, the earth, and all creation. He was lost in wonder and praise to the One who created all these things. By so doing, he gained a heart of wisdom and came to appreciate the greatness of the one true GOD! He discovered that God loves praise and worship. Whenever he worshiped, God's enveloping presence was tangible and the great joy and strength he felt were undeniable.

As a result, he developed a renowned lifestyle of praise and worship of God that made him stand out amongst others to the point of notice in the palace of King Saul! One of the servants said, "Look, I have seen a son of Jesse the Bethlehemite, who is skillful in playing, a mighty man of valor, a man of war, prudent in speech, and a handsome person; and the Lord is with him."

So David came to Saul and stood before him. And he loved him greatly, and he became his armorbearer.[19]

The secret of David's lifestyle was a genuine heart of love for God and this drove him to become skillful in playing his musical instruments. He would practice until he got the music piece right and enjoyed the glorious presence of God. With God's presence, he had great strength that enabled him to keep the sheep in the field from the attacks of the lion and the bear that came to prey on his territory. Such voracious animals attacking a teenager would have been tragic. It also would have been acceptable to lose some sheep, but not so with David. As an armorbearer in the service of his father, that was not an acceptable loss. He would stand against these predators boldly in victory!

For you to have success against the lions and the bears of this life, you will have to become who you really are. The bears and lions are the challenges of life that are sure to come to attack you in your territory, but when they come, you must face them with strength and boldness like David, becoming who you are, God's armorbearer!

ARMORBEARERS ARE SALT OF THE EARTH

As an armorbearer, you are salt of the earth and one of the primary roles of salt is to function as a flavoring agent, a seasoning that brings out the best in the food we eat.

"You are the salt of the earth; but if the salt loses its flavor, how shall it be seasoned? It is then good for nothing but to be thrown out and trampled underfoot by men."[20]

You are the world's seasoning that adds the God-flavors to this earth to bring out the best in it; without your input, it will be an intolerable place to live in. You have the responsibility to add value through your service to humanity by eliminating the tastelessness in your world.

The value of salt shows when it solves the problem of tastelessness. Until you embrace your purpose, your value will not show. You must seek to serve your generation and you begin with the closest circle of influence around you. When you serve selflessly in your role as husband, wife, homemaker, manager, or team leader, your value shows greatly and your usefulness brings joy and peace within that family, organization, community, or country.

Unfortunately, in our world today, we have the never-ending cycle of the *solution* complaining about the *problem* rather than embracing who they really are by solving the problem. When we refuse to embrace who we are as armorbearers in rendering service to the world we live in, then *'tastelessness'* will prevail.

The moral state of the world today is in shambles because those created to be salt of the earth are not embracing their respective roles and functions. Tastelessness has crept into our educational, social, and political systems, and sadly, even the church. Nowadays, we hear constantly through various news media of the sexual immorality and lack of financial and social accountability in these institutions and the devastating effect that has on so many lives, the majority being our children. We can change our world and eradicate this tastelessness. However, it must begin with us embracing who we really are, armorbearers.

As salt, you possess the attribute to preserve. Salt acts as a preservative by drawing out moisture from food so that disease-causing bacteria are unable to grow.

A lifestyle of service to your world allows you to stop the deterioration of the great quality of life God wants for all humanity. However, when we refuse to embrace our role and identity, chaos and instability will become rampant. Take at look at every rundown block and neighborhood in your city or in any city around the world, and you see the picture of what happens when you lose your flavor, when you fail to invest in who you really are in service and stewardship. You leave your world to decay and simply lose your usefulness and relevance in it.

ARMORBEARERS ARE LIGHT OF THE WORLD

As light, you possess the capacity to shine. The value light holds shows best in darkness. In the creation story, God saw a dark world and His solution to the darkness of the world was light![21]

"You are the light of the world. A city that is set on a hill cannot be hidden... Let your light so shine before men, that they may see your good works and glorify your Father in heaven."[22]

You are the solution to the darkness in the world today if only you will embrace your identity. Darkness always prevails in the absence of light. However once light appears, inevitably darkness must disappear. Darkness is helpless at the appearance of light because light disarms darkness.

Here's another way to put it: "You're here to be light, bringing out the God-colors in the world. God is not a secret to be kept. We're going public with this, as public as a city on a hill. If I make you light-bearers, you don't think I'm going to hide you under a bucket, do you? I'm putting you on a light stand. Now that I've put you there on a hilltop, on a light stand— shine! Keep open house; be generous with your lives. By opening up to others, you'll prompt people to open up with God, this generous Father in heaven."[23]

Nothing puts you in command when facing darkness like the light you carry. Armorbearers are light bearers! Armorbearing is all about shining as the light of the world in service to humanity. It begins with the understanding that you are light and that you have the responsibility to shine.

Your light will serve as a guide for others to see the right paths to walk. It will force a way through the darkness to expose the works of evil and ultimately destroy them.[24]

Light is extremely essential to growth and the sustenance of life on the earth! This means you really matter in the natural order of things. Your light shining bright along with the light of other armorbearers, makes one huge light that will never be put out.

Chapter Two

ARMORBEARING 101:
Developing the Spirit of an Armorbearer

*"Whoever desires to become great among you
shall be your servant. And whoever of you desires
to be first shall be slave of all."*[1]

THE PRICE OF ARMORBEARING

Two prominent brothers amongst the disciples of Jesus came to Him seeking a favor that would secure them a position of success, greatness, and significance. They asked, "Grant us that we may sit, one on Your right hand and the other on Your left, in Your glory." "Arrange it," they said, "so that we will be awarded the highest places of honor in Your glory."[2]

Both men had figured out the best route to the two most prestigious places in Jesus's administration or so they thought.

Sadly, many people are in similar positions today, trying to scheme their way to attain success in life. They erroneously think they have discovered the highway of *least resistance* and are speeding through with the false security that they have out-smarted everyone else. James and John thought the same.

Prior to their conversation with Jesus, the disciples argued about which of them would be the greatest. These brothers thought because of their close relationship with Jesus, they could maneuver their way onto the "two spots beside Him" and claim them as their own. They were confident that they would be the greatest, so they asked Jesus to endorse their opinion.

However, Jesus thwarted their plot with His response when He said, "to sit on My right hand and on My left is not Mine to give, but it is for those for whom it is prepared."[3]

By this statement, Jesus was not implying that He did not have the power to grant their request but was simply revealing the truth that there are no short cuts to greatness and significance in life.

Just as you cannot climb up a tree by starting from the top or clean a fish before you have caught it, you are unable to enjoy the benefits and blessings of greatness without first developing the virtues of an armorbearer. You must pay the price of armorbearing. Jesus reveals that God decides the place of dignity and position of greatness, and they are reserved only for those who embrace a lifestyle of service!

In order to be part of those for whom God has prepared the place of greatness and significance, you will have to qualify by developing the spirit and virtues of the armorbearer within you. Do not try to scheme your way up through short cuts; you must pay the price so you can gain the prize of greatness that God has prepared for you. When you resolve to give all it takes, then you will not be disappointed in your expectation.

Jesus said to His disciples, "You know that those who are considered rulers over the Gentiles lord it over them, and their great ones exercise authority over them. Yet it shall not be so among you."[4] He made this profound statement to show that true leadership or true greatness in the kingdom-of-God system is quite different from the way of the world.

True leadership is not in imposing and exercising the power and authority of a position; rather, it stems out of cultivating character and possessing the attitude of service. It is not in seeking self-glory, but in sacrifice.

If you are part of the kingdom-of-God system, you are not to operate the way the world does in substance and style, rather understand that true leadership and greatness come from developing the spirit of the armorbearer in you.

DESIRE TO BE GREAT

There are irrefutable virtues present in the life of an uncommon armorbearer; however, before you can obtain all these virtues, you must possess a strong inward desire to be great.

In resolving the dispute among His disciples, Jesus makes the statement, "Whoever desires to become great..."[5] to prove the truth that it all begins with desire. Jesus was saying it is a choice to make, not a gift to take.

The ability to become an uncommon armorbearer begins with desire. You must choose to pay the necessary price to cultivate what it takes to be an uncommon armorbearer. Until you resolve to pay the price, you cannot attain the status of armorbearer.

Desire is the seed for becoming what you want and the key for effective change. When desire comes, it is a tree of life.[6] In other words, you must nurture the "desire-seed" so that the tree of success can emerge, bearing the fruits of endless possibilities.

Desire is a strong feeling and irresistible inclination you have about the lack of satisfaction of where you are, which propels you to reach out for your ultimate goal.

It was desire that inspired the Wright brothers to fly.

It was desire that motivated Thomas Edison to persist through 10,000 experiments that failed before perfecting the incandescent light bulb. Henry Ford's unwavering desire revolutionized the automobile industry.[7]

So the question becomes, How intense is your desire? How much do you really want to become great? Will you nurture your "desire-seed" so it can grow and produce fruits of endless possibilities for you?

In his book *The Wisdom Commentary, Volume 2*, the great "wisdom-bank" and one of my valued mentors, Dr. Mike Murdock, states that *the proof of desire is in what you are willing to pursue.* He makes the point that you will always reach for what you really desire. Your desire will always make you go the extra mile, push a little harder, and reach a little higher. Citing as an example, the story in Mark 5:25–34, about the woman who was afflicted with an issue of blood for twelve years, and who had spent all her money on physicians, yet her condition had merely gotten worse; he states that the difference-maker was that she carried a seed of desire within her. She desired to be healed.

She chose to nurture that desire-seed; she touched the hem of Jesus's garment, and she was not disappointed. Immediately the fountain of her blood dried up, and she felt in her body that she was healed of the affliction. Her desire became the master of her need.[8]

Therefore, it is important to possess a strong desire and choose to cultivate that seed with determination; otherwise, success and greatness in life is not possible. Your great desire will help you overcome a multitude of natural deficiencies you may have and help sustain your commitment to your goals. As in the case of Bartimaeus Timaeus, a blind man who would not let anything stand in his way to get to Jesus, his great desire led to the restoration of his sight.[9]

The secret to having your desires fulfilled at all times is to delight in God. "Delight yourself in the Lord, and He shall give you the desires of your heart."[10]

So, what price must you pay?

1. PUT ON THE GRACE OF HUMILITY.

Humility is a great virtue possessed by every uncommon armorbearer. The opposite of humility is pride, arrogance, haughtiness, or boastfulness. It is virtually impossible to cultivate a lifestyle of genuine service with these impediments present in one's life.

"Let this same attitude and purpose and humble mind be in you, which was in Christ Jesus: Let Him be your example in humility."[11]

The dictionary defines humility as a way of behaving that shows that you do not think you are better or more important than other people.[12] This does not mean you are worthless or inferior; rather, it means that you place more value on others and recognize their worthy qualities.

Again, when Jesus said to His disciples, "You know that those who are considered rulers over the Gentiles lord it over them, and their great ones exercise authority over them. Yet it shall not be so among you."[13] He was saying that it would take humility to access the greatness they desired. Your willingness to humble yourself in dutiful service as an armorbearer determines the height of your rising in life. "Therefore humble yourselves under the mighty hand of God, that He may exalt you in due time."[14]

Great leaders of the Bible, like Moses, King David, and Jesus Christ are wonderful examples that show the lifting power of humility into greatness.

Apostle Paul reveals the truth about Jesus Christ who did not cling to the advantages and privileges of His status in divinity, but rather set all that aside and went through the humbling process in taking up the nature of a human though He is God. Because of this selfless act, Jesus received the greatest name ever, with such power that anything said by faith in His name will always happen![15]

In his book, *Celebration of Discipline*, Richard J Foster reminds us that "more than any other single way; the grace of humility is worked into our lives through the Discipline of service." He explains further that serving others, of all the classical spiritual disciplines, is the "most conducive to the growth of humility."[16]

So I challenge you to put on the grace of humility so you can grow and develop the seed and spirit of armorbearing within you.

2. YOU NEED THE STRENGTH OF FAITHFULNESS.

Another great virtue needed in the development of an uncommon armorbearer is faithfulness. This requirement is incontestable because without it your quest to develop into an effective armorbearer will be futile and unrewarding.

Faithfulness is defined as having or showing true and constant support, to be steadfast in allegiance, firm in adherence to observance of duty.[17] For you to serve your generation effectively you must set your heart in faithfulness to Him who called you.

Faithfulness is a requirement and not a choice. It is required in *armorbearers* that one is found faithful.[18] It is an expected duty, an indispensable necessity for you in order to excel in your quest.

Moses indeed was faithful in His entire house as a servant,[19] proving that every uncommon armorbearer understands that prioritizing this virtue is important to unlocking the benefits and blessings of servant-hood.

The uncommon armorbearer shows true and constant support for a legitimate cause or ministry, with un-wavering allegiance while bearing the call of duty un-til the goal is accomplished. He or she is committed to the assignment and consistent in the execution of any given task. This must become your lifestyle in order to gain the rewards because "a faithful man will abound with blessings."[20] When you invest in render-ing legitimate service, a fulfilled life of greatness and significance will be the result.

God found Abraham with this great virtue and in re-turn made a covenant with him; to give him the great-est real estate any man alive ever had, as a reward for his faithfulness.[21]

God has called you to Himself to serve faithfully in the ministry or industry He has placed you. It is not an optional choice but a sacred trust that you must obey and give an account. Therefore, faithfulness is an investment that will always yield a great dividend and establish you in a joyous and happy life.

In His illustration, Jesus said the kingdom of heaven is like a man going on a journey, who called his servants and entrusted his wealth to them. After a long time the master of those servants returned and settled accounts with them. The man who had received five bags of gold brought *an additional* five. "Master," he said, "you entrusted me with five bags of gold. See, I have gained five more." His master replied, "Well done, good and faithful servant! You have been faithful with a few things; I will put you in charge of many things. Come and share your master's happiness!"[22]

The rule of the game is faithfulness. Just as an Olympics athlete must play and compete by the rules; or else he loses out and is forced to give up his prized medal; the rewards and blessings of armorbearing depend greatly on faithfulness.[23]

3. THE VIRTUE OF INTEGRITY.

Integrity is the foundation upon which a great future

and lasting success stand. At the core of every great success is the virtue of integrity.

Integrity is the strength and depth of your character that allows you to live in truth, being honest with yourself and towards others. This establishes trust and respect in your lifestyle of service to others.

Integrity is the quality of being honest in your dealings and being morally upright. Your level of integrity determines the quality of your character. It is the height of your impact as an armorbearer because that is what will guide you to always *do the right thing,* in the right way, at the right time, and with the right motive in every situation. If you do the right thing, honesty will be your guide. But, if you are crooked, you will be trapped by your own dishonesty.[24]

The development of this great virtue of integrity is so important because you cannot afford for those you lead and serve to lose confidence in you. When people lose their confidence in you, your effectiveness as a leader withers and will cease eventually.

Jesus had a very short ministry lifespan of only three-and-a-half years; nevertheless, the impact of His ministry is still seen today over two thousand years later. There is not a whole lot written about His physical abilities but a lot about His integrity, and this is one of the true principles for success. In His time, Jesus lived in a society where prejudice, discrimination, immorality, and unrighteousness were the norm; nevertheless, He stood out in ministry because of His unwavering integrity.

You can stand out the same way by cultivating such integrity. Resolve always to tell the truth even at the expense of losing your life and be honest in all dealings. Make it your goal is to be blameless and above reproach. He who walks with integrity walks securely.[25] You must prize your integrity above all your relationships because this is the foundation for a great future and lasting success.

Integrity gives your word great value and gives your service great worth. Firmly decide to make this your invaluable character by consistent study of God's word, listening to preaching, and worship and prayer.

4. THE DISCIPLINE OF TEACHABILITY.

One of the greatest attributes of an uncommon armorbearer is teachability. To be teachable is to possess a willingness, drive, and passion for learning. This virtue is vital for the increase of your knowledge base, which in turn determines your rate of success in the race of life and your effectiveness in service.

Jesus Christ in His divinity still took it upon Himself to be teachable and to learn in various ways. On one of His many trips as a young boy with His parents, Mary and Joseph, the Bible says Jesus stayed behind in Jerusalem. Three days later, they found Jesus sitting in the temple, listening to the teachers and asking them questions.[26]

Though He was God in the flesh, He was still willing to learn the ways of men. He was twelve years old at the time and learned intensely because of the journey ahead. For an uncommon armorbearer, to possess the virtue of teachability is to be adequately equipped for any assigned tasks.

Armorbearing is a lifestyle of service, and as such it

is important to be vast in capacity so you can offer effective service by the maximum utilization of your abilities. Moreover, for this to happen, learning is vital. You must have the ability to soak up, like a dry sponge, every nugget of knowledge that will enhance your productivity and effectiveness. Your knowledge base determines your output rate.

The purpose of learning is not only to be properly equipped for service, but more importantly, it is for personal growth and development. The more growth and development you possess as an armorbearer, the more value you add to those around you. The value you add keeps you relevant in your area of influence.

THE COMPONENTS OF TEACHABILITY

There are two important components to teachability: listening and asking quality questions. Your ability to learn hangs on these. Jesus was in the temple *"listening to the teachers and asking them questions."*[27]

I. Learn to listen actively.

During their schooling experience, people mostly develop the skills of writing, reading, and speaking.

However, a majority do not develop the most valuable skill that enables our ability to learn—**LISTENING**!

A large number of people are unable to learn because they have not been taught the art of listening. A wise armorbearer must learn to listen so that learning can be an endless venture for growth and development.

LEARNING TO LISTEN ACTIVELY REQUIRES ATTENTION.
You must single-mindedly give concentrated attention to the person you are conversing with, and to what they are saying. Listen attentively to learn, as if you are about to hear a great secret that will be said only once. This shows you value the content of the conversation and it communicates to the person speaking that they are valuable. You must avoid interrupting, but rather take a few seconds to think and absorb the conversation before responding. By doing this, you are able to hear the actual message of the communication. No one can have faith without hearing the message.[28]

LEARNING TO LISTEN ACTIVELY REQUIRES ASKING QUESTIONS.
You must avoid assuming you already know what the

other person is trying to say. For clarification and understanding, it is important that you constantly ask questions. This communicates to the person speaking that you really care about what they are saying and you are committed to understanding the message. Seeking clarity and to understand their thoughts and feelings should be the purpose of the questions you ask others. With that, you are able to respond genuinely by demonstrating that you understand the message because you were really listening.

"Give instruction to a wise man, and he will be still wiser; teach a just man, and he will increase in learning."[29] Developing the art of listening as an armorbearer is one of the greatest skills that will equip you for effective service. Without it, you cannot serve God and humanity effectively.

II. ASK QUALITY QUESTIONS.

Your ability to ask quality questions will destroy every form of ignorance in your life and keep you on the fast track of learning. Ignorance produces continuous loss in your life because you have not discovered the discipline of asking quality questions.[30] The greatest discoveries in our world today were made by people who asked the right questions, and they unlocked the golden doors to their uncommon success.

Quality questions are like seeds—when planted, they bring forth a tree of fruits. In order to keep learning, you must ask quality questions.[31] If you want to know what God wants you to do, ask Him, and He will gladly tell you, for He is always ready to give a bountiful supply of wisdom to all who ask Him; He will not resent it. But when you ask Him, be sure that you really expect Him to tell you, for a doubtful mind will be as unsettled as a wave of the sea that is driven and tossed by the wind. Every decision you then make will be uncertain, as you turn first this way and then that. If you don't ask with faith, don't expect the Lord to give you any solid answer.[32]

Asking quality questions will unlock new seasons, new levels, and new knowledge for you. It will schedule new events on the earth for you as an armorbearer so you can fulfill your assignment of service.

5. SACRIFICIAL LOVE-WORK IS REQUIRED

Without a true and genuine heart of love, effective servanthood is unattainable and armorbearing has no value.

God loved the people of this world so much that He gave His only Son *in service to humanity*, so that everyone who has faith in Him will have eternal life and never really die.[33] Therefore it is your love for God that gives you a heart to serve humanity.

What does the Lord your God require of you? He requires only that you fear the Lord your God, and live in a way that pleases Him, and love Him and serve Him with all your heart and soul.[34] He wants you to serve from a heart that is powered by love.

In developing the spirit of an armorbearer, the sacrifice of love is required. Love is sacrificing self in order to ensure the wellbeing of another. Without a loving heart, the love-walk and love-work are impossible. A loving heart is the foundation for real armorbearing.

Love is not a feeling or an emotion. Love is work!

Love is a verb! Love is action! Love is a decision! Love is making the choice to be patient, kind, humble, respectful, selfless, forgiving, honest, and committed.[35] Without love, uncommon armorbearing is not possible. Your love-walk empowers you for effective love service that makes a difference in your generation.

Moses loved the people of Israel and so served them effectively.[36] David also served his generation effectively because of his love-walk.[37] Other examples of uncommon armorbearers in recent generations that were powered by their loving heart were people like Nelson Mandela, Mohandas "Mahatma" Gandhi, Martin Luther King, Jr., Mother Teresa, and Abraham Lincoln.

NELSON MANDELA was an anti-apartheid revolutionary who went on to serve as the first black president of South Africa from 1994 to 1999. A noted human rights activist, Mandela led South Africa's fight against segregation and apartheid.

MOHANDAS "MAHATMA" GANDHI led the *nationalist* fight for Indian *independence* against British rule in the 1920s. His celebrated use of nonviolent protest inspired similar movements in support of *human* rights and freedoms around the globe. "Mahatma," which translates to "venerable" in Sanskrit, was an honorific first bestowed on him in 1914 in South Africa, and is now widely used.

MARTIN LUTHER KING, JR. was an American activist and humanitarian who became the leader of the African—American Civil Rights Movement. Similar to Mahatma Gandhi, King became known for advancing civil rights through nonviolent civil disobedience. As a Baptist minister, King took part in the 1955 Montgomery Bus Protest, a political and social campaign against the racially segregated public transit system in Montgomery, *Alabama.* King went on to help organize the 1963 March on Washington, where he famously delivered his iconic "I Have a Dream" speech.

MOTHER TERESA was an Albanian-born Roman Catholic nun. In 1950 she founded the Missionaries of Charity in Calcutta, India, a religious congregation that is currently active in more than 130 countries. In her work with the Missionaries of Charity, Mother Teresa cared for the poor, sick, orphaned, and dying.

The Missionaries of Charity gradually expanded beyond India, and in 2012 consisted of more than 4,500 sisters operating in 133 countries. The congregation runs hospices and homes for people with HIV, leprosy, and tuberculosis; *it also operates* soup kitchens; children's and family counseling programs; *and* orphanages and schools.

ABRAHAM LINCOLN was the sixteenth president of the United States, and led the country through the tumultuous American Civil War, fought from 1861 to 1865. The war, fought over the contentious issue of slavery, began after several Southern states moved to secede, and formed the Confederate States of America.

Lincoln's Gettysburg Address, delivered on November 19, 1863, during the Civil War, is one of the best-known speeches in American history. In it, Lincoln echoed the principles of human equality from the Declaration of Independence, and declared that the Civil War, and the preservation of the Union, would bring true equality to all the country's citizens.

Lincoln's efforts to abolish slavery culminated in the Emancipation Proclamation, which was issued on January 1, 1863. The measure prompted the Senate to pass the Thirteenth Amendment to the United States Constitution, which permanently outlawed slavery.[38]

These great armorbearers' love-work earned them the distinction of truly changing the world, to prove the power of love in the effectiveness of service.

You must be positioned in love before you can play your armorbearing role well because without it your capacity to serve others well will be greatly diminished. The people you do not love, you will not have the real capacity to serve them well.

Your love-walk and love-work enable you as an armorbearer to conquer any challenging mountainous situations you may encounter in your quest to fulfill your assignment. The good news is that love never fails![39] This implies that nothing will be impossible for you when your service to God and humanity is powered by love.

For example, Daniel enjoyed access to God's divine secrets that helped him solve national problems in Babylon simply because of his loving heart.[40]

With sacrificial love-work, you will never be confused or intimidated to take steps in the face of challenging circumstances. There is no fear in love. On the contrary, love that has achieved its goal gets rid of fear, because fear has to do with punishment; the person who keeps fearing has not been brought to maturity in regard to love.[41]

Chapter Three

ARMORBEARING 102
Developing the Soul of an Armorbearer

"If anyone desires to come after Me,
let him deny himself, and take up his cross daily,
and follow Me."[1]

THE COST OF ARMORBEARING

SELF-SACRIFICE: *"LET HIM DENY HIMSELF..."*

Jesus Christ, the greatest armorbearer that ever walked the earth, said anyone willing to walk in His footsteps must bear the cost of self-sacrifice. He said this is the prescribed way to live, His way, the only way to finding one's true self.

Self-sacrifice is the denial of personal interests and needs in order to serve others or advance a cause.

"I do not seek My own will," Jesus said, "but the will of the Father who sent Me."[2] It is not about getting your own way, it is about carrying out orders. You must have the willingness to give up your rights and privileges in order to satisfy the legitimate needs of people.

A self-sacrificing mentality indicates that you are "other people" minded in your disposition toward life, thereby making a desirable difference in the lives of many. You are indifferent about your position or status but more concerned about how you can make significant contributions to the advancement and progress of others.

Self-sacrifice also means you willingly come under authority in order to exercise authority. It means that your personal self-will has no bearing whatsoever. Rather, God's will takes precedence in your life. You will have to lay down your will under the command of God for you to be able to command authority in service. A life of absolute surrender is required for self-sacrifice.

Once making this case about Jesus, one of the great apostles of the Bible said to "Think of yourselves the way Christ Jesus thought of Himself. He had equal status with God but did not think so much of Himself that He had to cling to the advantages of that status no matter what. Not at all. When the time came, He set aside the privileges of deity and took on the status of a slave, became human! Having become human, He stayed human. It was an incredibly humbling process. He did not claim special privileges. Instead, He lived a selfless (self-sacrificing), obedient life."[3]

Jesus said of Himself, "I am the Good Shepherd. I know My own sheep and My own sheep know Me. In the same way, the Father knows Me and I know the Father. I put the sheep before Myself, sacrificing Myself."[4] So you must pay the price just like Jesus did and lay down your rights and privileges, your status and dignity, then put on the garment of service. This is the way to become truly great!

Jesus said it best, "Anyone wanting to be the greatest must be the least—the servant of all!"[5]

SELF-DISCIPLINE: *"TAKE UP HIS CROSS DAILY..."*
The word *cross* speaks of your assignment or sphere of service to humanity as assigned by God. It is the place where you die to self and devote to service. So taking up your cross is the call to recognize your unique sphere of service and embrace the responsibility it demands. It takes self-discipline to take up your cross daily.

Discipline is the skill of doing what you are supposed to do, when you are supposed to do it, and how you are supposed to do it, regardless of how you feel.

Self-discipline allows you to embrace the demand of the service required and fulfill it without falling to the deportment of your personal mood or situation. With self-discipline, every other principle that makes for successful armorbearing will work, but without it, none of them will work.

Self-discipline is crucial to your greatness. It opens doors of opportunities and makes things work for you. With self-discipline, the average person can rise as far and as fast as his talents and intelligence can take him or her. But without self-discipline, a person with every blessing of background, education and opportunity will seldom rise above mediocrity.[6]

Apostle Paul, one of the greatest and most prolific writers in Bible history, stated, "Don't you know that all the runners in the stadium run, but only one gets the prize? So run to win. Everyone who competes practices self-discipline in everything.[7]

Self-discipline is required in thoughts, behavior, emotions, reactions, speech, and inclinations. It is required in everything because it is the foundation for a lifelong success as an armorbearer, and without it, you will not get very far!

SELF-IMPROVEMENT: *"FOLLOW ME."*
Jesus is the model for the uncommon armorbearer. When He said, "follow Me," He meant follow His example. "Even the Son of Man did not come for people to serve Him. He came to serve others and to give His life to save many people."[8]

You must become someone who is learning His
(Jesus) way of doing things and in the process, you
daily improve in the quality and level of your service.
Your ability to improve by adding value to yourself
will determine the quality and rating of your servanthood.

Personal development is essential for you to become a
valued armorbearer in your sphere of service. This way
you continue to make a lasting difference in the lives
of people. It will help you remain relevant and on the
cutting edge in our constantly changing world.

In ancient times, the servant who was unskilled and
undeveloped rarely lasted in service, because to avoid
waste, his master would either sell him for much less
value or have him killed.   On the other hand, developed and skillful servants are precious and preserved
at all cost by their masters. If the servant got sick, his
master would do whatever it took to get him well.[9]
These uncommon servants were placed in positions
of responsibility and authority, while some of them
eventually gained their freedom or became masters as
well.

For example, in Bible history, Abraham's oldest servant was developed and skilled to the point that he was the designated heir prior to the birth of Abraham's son. In addition, at some point, this man had the responsibility to find a wife for Abraham's son from among his relatives.[10]

The Bible says that, while a servant in the house of Potiphar in Egypt, Joseph was a successful man. Potiphar was so impressed with his administrative skills that he put Joseph in charge of his whole family organization.[11]

The importance of personal development and self-improvement cannot be overstated—because without it, you cannot stand out in effectiveness and quality of service. You remain relevant and valuable when you keep growing and improving. You must be intentional about your development by committing to learning something new every day, reading books and attending seminars and webinars. Whatever the medium, you must commit to growing daily so you can remain an effective armorbearer.

Chapter Four
ARMORBEARING 103
The Process of Transformation

*"Come out from among them
and be separate…"[1]*

PAYING THE PRICE OF ARMORBEARING

CONSECRATION

Consecration means to be set apart for uncommon service as an armorbearer in the sphere of influence that God has placed you. Consecration is the sanctification of your life by setting it apart as dedicated to God. It is the serious commitment to your God-given purpose.

Jesus Christ our greatest example of armorbearing recognized early in life as a young boy that He had to be in His Father's business.[2] He understood at this tender age that God consecrated Him to run with the heavenly agenda on the earth, not to seek His own will or to advance His own interests. Jesus had no desire to please Himself. He said, "I do not seek My own will but the will of the Father who sent me."[3]

Jesus found His fulfillment in doing the will of God and completing the work assigned to Him. He was unlike the other community children who ran around playing all day, rather He gave Himself completely to His assignment without wavering and without losing focus.

As a Christian armorbearer, there is a need for consecration if success and greatness is your goal. Consecration strengthens your faith, and grants you access to divine insights and revelations on the great plans God has for humanity.

The price of total commitment to a life of service is essential. It requires singleness of mind and focus on your assignment of serving while being undeterred by the accompanying challenges that come because of the role you play. Joseph is a prime example of a man seriously committed to his God-given purpose of armorbearing. He resolved not to be distracted by the opportunity to enjoy preferential access into the arms of the first lady of the house.

Joseph was a strikingly handsome man, but as time went on, his master's wife became infatuated with *him* and one day *she* said, "Sleep with me." He wouldn't do it. He said to his master's wife, "Look, with me here, my master doesn't give a second thought to anything that goes on here—he's put me in charge of everything he owns. He treats me as an equal. The only thing he hasn't turned over to me is you. You're his wife, after all! How could I violate his trust and sin against God?"[4]

Joseph's refusal was the price of consecration he had to pay because he was focused on his divine assignment. Although he was incarcerated for his actions, after a series of life-events Joseph eventually ascended to the executive role of vice president of the whole nation.

By paying the price of consecration you can maintain the integrity of your mission of service without losing sight of what is most important. We hear frequently in the news today of many people in high positions in government, businesses and even churches caught in various scandals simply because they failed to pay the price of consecration. They compromised the integrity of their mission of service and betrayed the trust of the people.

To become an uncommon armorbearer, you must pay the price of consecration. The good news is that Jesus Christ has already fulfilled the ultimate requirement so you can appropriate it daily through a life of total surrender. This requires a passion for doing what you say you are going to do, following through on promises, and finishing what you began. You need the passion for doing the right thing and being the best you can be. It requires a passion for helping others along their journey to be the best they can be.[5] Dwight Lyman Moody[6] puts it this way, "The world has yet to see what God can do with a man fully consecrated to him. By God's help, I aim to be that man."

COMPASSION

Compassion is the feeling of wanting to help someone who is in need. It allows you to see beyond the immediate and have a deep awareness of the lost, the hurting, the suffering, the distressed, and the needy so you can genuinely care for and serve others. It demands that you pay attention to the details of events that happen around you so you can notice the potential areas of service, and truly identify the legitimate needs of people who require your help.

Jesus went about all the cities and villages, teaching in their synagogues, preaching the gospel of the kingdom, and healing every sickness and every disease among the people. But when He saw the multitudes, He was moved with compassion for them, because they were weary and scattered, like sheep having no shepherd.[7]

Compassion gives you the ability to render *heart service* rather than *eye-service*, and helps you genuinely connect with those you serve. People that have made tremendous impacts in past generations accomplished this mainly because they were compassionate. It took them to where the people were, so they could feel their hurt and pain, and thus they were propelled to render the appropriate solutions and service.

Compassion requires you to be on the lookout for ways to help others. When you see a need, you must take responsibility by quickly seizing the moment to do something about it because opportunities to serve sometimes often do not last long. You must take advantage of every opportunity you get to serve. "Therefore, as we have opportunity, let us do good to all, especially to those who are of the household of faith."[8]

GRATITUDE

Gratitude is an essential price to pay because while embracing your role as armorbearer, you are not always going to be comfortable, especially if you are just starting out. Armorbearing will stretch you and keep you on the road less traveled, but you must always be grateful to God every moment of the way if you are going to survive the journey.

Jonah was a political lover of the nation of Israel and a committed patriot, who God sent as His armorbearer with a message of repentance and mercy to preach to Nineveh, a gentile city. This was a very uncomfortable assignment for Jonah because he found it difficult to accept the fact that God would show grace and mercy to such a city when they deserved severe judgment. His initial disobedience to God's instruction turned into a reluctant uncomfortable obedience. However, in great misery he decided to wait to see if the appointed Day of Judgment would take place.

"So Jonah went out of the city and sat on the east side. The LORD God prepared a plant and made it come up over Jonah, that it might be shade for his head to deliver him from his misery. So Jonah was very grateful for the plant."[9]

Jonah's gratitude for the plant allowed God to show him the concern He should have for the city of Nineveh and the love God has for all men.

Gratitude is the battery that keeps the flow of divine insight and revelation for excellence in service.

It allows you to tap into the unseen realms of possibilities when faced with great challenges in the course of your service.

The challenges of armorbearing are highly demanding. However they are always bearable if one embraces a lifestyle of gratitude. Here are some examples of the challenges you might face as an armorbearer but which you can overcome through gratitude.

THE CHALLENGE OF CRITICISM:

GRATEFUL ARMORBEARERS HANDLE CRITICISM WELL.
Criticism is the act of passing undue or severe judgment on someone. It is the act of finding fault and judging someone unfavorably and harshly.

In the execution of your service within your sphere of influence, you will encounter people who are critical of you. You will experience harsh words and verbal abuses unduly that will pierce like arrows, but a heart of gratitude allows you to remember that service is a privilege, not a right. You will gain the understanding that criticism comes with the job and taking it personally will only distract you from your mission.

Mary of Bethany, the sister of Lazarus and Martha, was someone who served Jesus wholeheartedly; however, people criticized her for it. She came while Jesus was eating, with a beautiful alabaster jar filled with expensive perfume from India that was made of pure *nard*. Now, it was customary to anoint the guests heads with a small smudge amount of oil when they arrived for a meal, but Mary went beyond the traditional ceremonial greeting with Jesus. Opening the jar, she poured the entire contents on His head. This was an extravagant expression of her service and devotion to Jesus. For this, Jesus commended her highly because her act was so precious and symbolic of His imminent death. This perceptive act proved that Mary listened and believed in Jesus and His teachings in a more intimate way than all the other disciples. She showed Him special honor as a gift in preparation for His burial. Unfortunately, this made some of the guests angry and they criticized her sharply, stating she had wasted the perfume oil that was worth a full year's paycheck.

Mary handled the criticism well because of her heart of gratitude for Jesus's impact in her life. Her expression of gratitude was higher in scale and untouched by the intensity of the harsh critical words spoken against her. In response, Jesus sealed her greatness and enduring significance worldwide by saying, "Wherever this gospel is preached in the whole world, what this woman has done will also be told as a memorial to her."[10]

Unlike the disciples who longed and lobbied for fame and fortune in Jesus's kingdom, Mary entered into the benefit of lasting significance because she loved and served as an uncommon armorbearer with a heart of gratitude.

THE CHALLENGE OF LONELINESS:

GRATEFUL ARMORBEARERS RISE ABOVE LONELINESS.

As an armorbearer entrusted with the mission of uncommon service, you are required to be ahead, to blaze the trail and set the pace. This is a lonely pathway. The good news, however, is that you may be lonely on this journey but you are never alone.

We discussed earlier about David, who was in the wilderness by himself tending his father's sheep. However, he realized that he was not alone because the presence of God was there with him. He discovered how to "woo" God with his music and gained strength through the joy he derived from being in His presence, which empowered him to overcome the attacks from the lion and the bear that came against his father's flock. He faced the giant Goliath and gained victory because he had a solid backing.

When you are in God, you are never alone. He said, "It is not good for man to be alone."[11] In your lonely moments, intentionally put your focus on God and the reality of His presence, and you will find strength to stay on track with the assignment of armorbearing. Learn to use your *aloneness* to grow and develop yourself in God. Jesus often went to lonely places by himself to pray. He had the reality of the ever-abiding presence of the Father around Him always. One time He said, "Indeed the hour is coming, yes, has now come, that you will be scattered, each to his own, and will leave me alone. And yet I am not alone, because the Father is with Me.[12]

Understand that greatness is a process and every experience of emptiness and loneliness simply prepares you for the great fulfillment of your purpose and destiny. Keep the image of a great and glorious future; see yourself making a difference in the lives of people, and you will gain the wisdom and insight needed to win every battle of life. You are not alone. "There is a friend who sticks closer than a brother."[13] Be grateful every moment and step of the way because your gratitude will lift you above every challenge of loneliness into your next level.

THE CHALLENGE OF FATIGUE:

GRATEFUL ARMORBEARERS OVERCOME FATIGUE.

Effective armorbearing requires you to face the challenge of fatigue because servanthood places heavy demands on the armorbearer. Everyone is looking for strength in every armorbearer to handle the demands and responsibilities of the position. Frankly, it can be stressful at times. This is why Moses told his armorbearer, Joshua, to "be strong,"[14] and Paul told his armorbearer, Timothy, to "be strong."[15] They made these charges because it is not possible to be unaffected by the physical, emotional, and mental demands of effective service as an uncommon armorbearer.

Your grateful attitude will make the flow of supernatural strength available to you; to help dispel the stress and fatigue generated by running with the demands of service. Along with your attitude of gratitude, you must incorporate a lifestyle of disciplined physical exercise, a healthy eating plan, and taking scheduled rests to avoid becoming a victim of fatigue.

Even Jesus found cause to increase in His physical stature[16] and on many occasions took time away with His disciples from serving the crowd to rest. He said, "Let's go off by ourselves to a quiet place and rest awhile." He made this statement because there were so many people coming and going that Jesus and his apostles didn't even have time to eat.[17]

Jesus reveals that as an armorbearer, you can burn brightly without burning out! Your willingness to bear the challenge of fatigue in the discharge of your role is proof that you are developing as an uncommon armorbearer.

Maintain a lifestyle of gratitude to God to keep the flow of supernatural strength coming your way.

THE CHALLENGE OF REJECTION:

GRATEFUL ARMORBEARERS OVERCOME REJECTION.

This is one of the most common challenges of an armorbearer. The dictionary definition of rejection is the refusal to accept, approve, or support something or someone.

If you are willing to embrace the call to servanthood in your sphere of influence, you must be willing to experience non-acceptance, disapproval, lack of support, and misunderstanding from those you are called to serve. Jesus came to His own people, and even they rejected Him.[18]

Grateful armorbearers effect change whether they are accepted or not, whether they are appreciated or not. They understand that it is a privilege to have the opportunity to serve and not a right.

Just because you experience rejection does not mean that you are doing things wrong. Someone once said, "No one is ever fully accepted until he is first, utterly rejected." The truth remains that you can bounce back from rejection. Referring to Jesus, the Bible says the stone which the builders rejected has become the chief cornerstone.[19] The stone the builders rejected as worthless, good for nothing, turned out to be the most important of all! This is true of every grateful uncommon armorbearer.

It is important that you do not let rejection affect you negatively, instead choose never to lose your heart of gratitude. Keep your focus on the ultimate objective of making a difference when faced with the challenges that come with service. This way, you will not be affected by the immediate effects of rejection.

Chapter Five
ARMORBEARING 104
Four Kinds of Servants

"Servants, obey your boss in everything.
Obey always, not only when he is looking at you
as if you were pleasing a man. Do it with all
your heart because you respect the Lord."[1]

Everyone serves in one capacity or another. Some serve for a worthwhile cause, while others serve for their own selfish agenda. In any case, everyone who serves falls under one of four kinds of servants and each bears its corresponding levels of reward.

#1. PASSIVE SERVANTS–ARMOR-BARRIERS
Passive servants are people who only render service when it is convenient for them. They do not give their best effort in service and turn a deaf ear when re-

quired to give more. Passive servants complain when their personal effort does not produce the results they desire. They expect everyone else to produce success for them. As a result, they are *barriers* to their own progress and the progress of others. They hinder the productivity of others because of their inability to give concerted effort that raises the quality of service they render. They accept the status quo and have no desire to change since they possess only a halfhearted commitment to the responsibility of service. This lukewarm approach to service only culminates in uselessness.

God said to a church of passive servants: "I know your works, that you are neither cold nor hot. I could wish you were cold or hot. So then, because you are lukewarm, and neither cold nor hot, I will vomit you out of My mouth.[2]

Judas was so close to greatness in Jesus, but out of greed, he lost the opportunity to impact the world through Jesus's ministry. In a moment of selfish convenience, he betrayed Jesus for thirty pieces of silver. Needless to say, his life ended tragically.[3]

A passive approach to service will only strip you of your opportunity to make a difference in the lives of people and disqualify you as a beneficiary of the rewards of service.

#2. PARASITE SERVANTS–ARMOR-BORERS

Parasite servants are people who serve only to pursue credibility so they can gain recognition. They enjoy taking advantage of people and situations simply for personal gain. When people serve in this capacity, they steal the credit for the accomplishments of others because they cannot achieve anything on their own efforts. Parasite servants are lazy people who love the limelight, and love being the center of attention. They love getting from other people by controlling and diverting the flow of information, but never benefiting the people they serve.

Parasite servants exploit and abuse others for their personal advantage. They become unhappy when denied their source of nourishment. This puts a hole within the team or organization they are a part of and undermines the effectiveness of their service as a whole. They wrongly want praise, glory, and reputation but eventually lose all because they never give their best in service.

Armor-borers use the influence and prestigious name of leaders to manipulate others into a relationship for their sole advantage. They are people-pleasers who serve with the wrong motives and never end well in life because they render service to take rather than to give.

Haman was a royal officer in the courts of King Ahasuerus. He used his position of authority to plot the destruction of all the Jews in the kingdom, as vengeance against Mordecai who refused to bow and pay homage to him.[4] Unfortunately, Haman's elaborate plan to have the king hang Mordecai on the gallows turned against him. He was hanged instead, while Modecai was honored.[5]

After two full years of service to the Ephesians, Paul in his farewell message said, "Servants, be obedient to those who are your physical masters, having respect for them and eager concern to please them, in singleness of motive and with all your heart, as service to Christ Himself— not in the way of eye-service as if they were watching you and only to please men, but as servants of Christ, doing the will of God heartily and with your whole soul; rendering service readily with goodwill, as to the Lord and not to men."[6]

#3. PRODIGAL SERVANTS–ARMOR-BREAKERS
Prodigal servants are people who are recklessly wasteful in their mode of service. They enjoy showing off extravagantly at the expense of everyone else, squandering every available resource intended for the benefit of all.

The prodigal son was impatient to serve his father for the length of time required for an heir. He demanded from his father, "Father, I want right now what's coming to me." Not long after, he packed his bags and left home with his share of the inheritance. "Undisciplined and dissipated, he wasted everything he had.[7]

Armor-breakers complain frequently and enjoy making excuses for their incompetence. Their self-aggrandizing approach to service, coupled with their need for showmanship, makes the outcome of whatever they are involved in wasteful and destructive. The wise king Solomon said, "He also that is slothful in his work is brother to him that is a great waster."[8] Armor-breakers lack the strength of character to stay the cause of the mission because they want to satisfy an unhealthy, lavish lifestyle. When difficulty arises, they change camps quickly. They are undependable people and very lazy in regard to work.

#4. PRODUCTIVE SERVANTS–ARMOR-BEARERS

Productive servants are people who take on the responsibility of service as a privilege to make a positive difference in the lives of others. They are selfless in their approach to service and always willing to invest their best to get the job done.

Elisha served Elijah as an armorbearer. He left everything to follow Elijah and became his servant.[9] Just before God took Elijah, Elisha's loyalty was tested three times, but each time, he declared his unwavering commitment to Elijah, "As the Lord lives, and as your soul lives, I will not leave you!"[10]

Jonathan served David as an armorbearer. He said to David, "Tell me what you have in mind, I'll do anything for you."[11] Jonathan stood up for David before his father, Saul, and stood by him in distressing times. He was selfless, willing to risk being at odds with his father just to save David. Jonathan loved David more than his own soul.[12]

Ruth served Naomi as an armorbearer. After the death of Naomi's husband and two sons, she urged her daughters-in-law, Ruth and Orpah, to return to their mother's house. Orpah after some persuasion returned home, but Ruth decided to stick with Naomi. In selflessness, she told Naomi, "Don't force me to leave you; don't make me go home. Where you go, I go; and where you live, I'll live–not even death itself is going to come between us!"[13]

These uncommon armorbearers exemplify true humility and love in their service duties. They possess the strength of faithfulness to stick to the task until it is completed. Productive servants have the impeccable virtue of integrity; they are willing to learn new ways to improve and deliver quality service at the highest standards. These people daily bear the cost and pay the price of servanthood to the full; moreover, they render their work with an attitude of gratitude and appreciation.

Productive servants serve wholeheartedly and get to enjoy the full rewards of servanthood! They understand that true armorbearing is not eye-service, nor is it subservience, slavery, or self-serving. Rather, they see it as a practical orientation toward a lifestyle of genuine love for God and a heart for meeting the legitimate needs of people.

Chapter Six
ARMORBEARING 105
The Rewards of Armorbearing

"And behold, I am coming quickly,
and My reward is with Me, to give to every one
according to his work."[1]

"Each man's work will one day be shown for what it is. The day will show it plainly enough, for the day will arise in a blaze of fire, and that fire will prove the nature of each man's work. If the work that the man has built upon the foundation will stand this test, he will be rewarded. But if a man's work be destroyed under the test, he loses it all."[2.]

It is important to note that God will prove your heart in service before He raises you up to enjoy the rewards.   He does it so He can expose the true motive behind your servanthood. (We see this proof in the lives of Joseph, Joshua, and Jesus). Many people today serve for different reasons, but the kind of service that's rewarded is that which is according to God's prescription.

"But I, the Lord, search all hearts and examine secret motives. I give all people their due rewards, according to what their actions deserve."[3] Further, "God pays people back for what they have done and gives them what their actions deserve."[4]

The picture that Matthew 7:22–23 paints reveals this unparalleled truth: it is not enough just to render service but to serve according to the terms prescribed by God. *"Many will say to Me in that day, 'Lord, Lord, have we not prophesied in Your name, cast out demons in Your name, and done many wonders in Your name?' And then I will declare to them, 'I never knew you; depart from Me, you who practice lawlessness!'"*

Jesus said many people will come to Him on the day of rewards, when judging everyone's service, to say to Him that they did great humanitarian services, wonderful health care drives and grand benevolence outreaches; but they would not be rewarded nor recognized for all "the service rendered" simply because the motive and object of their services were for self and not for His glory. Though wonderful deeds were accomplished, they will all mean nothing without the proper foundation. The service you render as an armorbearer is like building a house, and the foundation determines if it stands or falls.

To enjoy the true rewards of a lifestyle of service, your connection to God through His son, Jesus Christ is the primary requirement. Research reveals that ninety percent of the current motivational books and resources take their roots straight from the Bible yet many who have been great facilitators of progress and success do not care to acknowledge God. Though these resources have helped many people, many of these authors do not have any connection with Him. These people are anonymous to the most important Person of all. They are unaware that it is through our connection to Him by faith that our eternal reward for a lifestyle of service is secured.

Without a connection to Him, all the great services rendered prove nothing because God will say, "I never knew you." Therefore, an armorbearer serving according to the rules is what will guarantee the best rewards.

Once connectivity with God is established, your disposition to a lifestyle of service must be according to the following rules as prescribed by God. These are the rules that define the code of service and the rewards of the uncommon armorbearer.

THE ARMORBEARER'S CODE OF SERVICE

I. THE ARMORBEARER MUST SERVE **ACCEPTABLY**.
"Therefore, since we are receiving a kingdom which cannot be shaken, let us have grace, by which we may serve God acceptably..."[5]

II. THE ARMORBEARER MUST SERVE **RIGHTEOUSLY**.
And Solomon said: "You have shown great mercy to Your servant David my father, because he walked before You in truth, in righteousness, and in uprightness of heart with You."[6]

III. THE ARMORBEARER MUST SERVE **WILLINGLY**.

"For if I preach the gospel, I have nothing to boast of, for necessity is laid upon me; yes, woe is me if I do not preach the gospel! For if I do this willingly, I have a reward; but if against my will, I have been entrusted with a stewardship."[7]

IV. THE ARMORBEARER MUST SERVE **CHEERFULLY**.

"Serve the Lord cheerfully. Come into His presence with a joyful song."[8]

V. THE ARMORBEARER MUST SERVE **WHOLEHEARTEDLY**.

"Serve wholeheartedly, as if you were serving the Lord, not people."[9]

VI. THE ARMORBEARER MUST SERVE **DILIGENTLY**.

"But whatever I am now, it is all because God poured out His special favor on me—and not without results. For I have worked harder than any of the other apostles; yet it was not I but God who was working through me by His grace."[10]

VII. THE ARMORBEARER MUST SERVE **FAITHFULLY**.

"Let a man so consider us, as servants of Christ and

stewards of the mysteries of God. Moreover it is required in stewards that one be found faithful."[11]

VIII. THE ARMORBEARER MUST SERVE **SACRIFICIALLY.**
"Your faith makes you offer your lives as a sacrifice in serving God."[12] Furthermore, "This is how we've come to understand and experience love: Christ sacrificed His life for us. This is why we ought to live sacrificially for our fellow believers, and not just be out for ourselves."[13]

IX. THE ARMORBEARER MUST SERVE **TIRELESSLY.**
"Epaphras, who is one of you, says hello. What a trooper he has been! He's been tireless in his prayers for you, praying that you'll stand firm, mature and confident in everything God wants you to do."[14] Also, "Don't get tired of helping others. You will be rewarded when the time is right, if you don't give up."[15]

X. THE ARMORBEARER MUST SERVE **REVERENTLY.**
The acceptable way to serve God is in reverential fear and with a heart of gratitude for the opportunity because of your genuine love for Him. "Serve the Lord with reverent awe and worshipful fear; rejoice and

be in high spirits with trembling lest you displease Him."[16]

THE REWARDS OF A LIFESTYLE OF SERVICE

When you serve according to the rules; according to the code of service, there is a guarantee of rewards. You have the promise that your reward will be exponentially above what you sacrificed and put in while serving. For He repays man according to his work, And makes man to find a reward according to his way.[17]

Peter said, "We've left our homes to follow you." "Yes," Jesus replied, "and I assure you that everyone who has given up house or wife or brothers or parents or children, for the sake of the Kingdom of God, will be repaid many times over in this life, and will have eternal life in the world to come."[18]

Jesus's reply to Peter reveals that it is quite profitable and rewarding to serve God. The greatest investment to make is to serve God and His cause on the earth because it yields the greatest dividend of greatness and lasting success. You must choose to make this investment on three main platforms in other to get the full reward:

I. SERVE GOD WITH YOUR TIME.

Serving God with your time falls under two divisions, the time of your life and the time of your days. The time of your life is defined by your *biological clock*, your age. You must serve God wherever you are on this clock, while young and while old. You are never too young and cannot get too old to serve God. "God told me, 'Don't say, "I'm only a boy." I'll tell you where to go and you'll go there. I'll tell you what to say and you'll say it. Don't be afraid of a soul. I'll be right there, looking after you.'"[19]

"Now there was one Anna, a prophetess… this woman was a widow of about eighty-four years, who did not depart from the temple, but served God with fasting and prayers night and day."[20]

The time of your days is defined by your *mechanical clock*. Jesus said "I must work the works of Him who sent Me while it is day; the night is coming when no one can work."[21] Out of your alloted twenty-four hours per day, you must commit to use a portion of that time in service to the cause of God on the earth. Use your time the best way you can; serve in your church, in your community, and in your country.

II. SERVE GOD WITH YOUR TALENTS AND GIFTS.

There are natural endowments God put in everyone He created and you are not exempt. There is something unique about you, something you do effortlessly that would be a struggle for someone else to do. This is a pointer to your talent.

For example, a naturally tall person did absolutely nothing to be tall, it is simply a gift from God. This is his natural endowment and he can use that in service to God. Whatever results and advantages his height brings can be used in the advancement of God's cause on the earth.

"A man's gift makes room for him and brings him before great men."[22] The same must be with you because God has endowed everyone with special abilities, talents, and gifts.

"Each one has his own gift from God, one in this manner and another in that."[23]

III. SERVE GOD WITH YOUR TREASURE.

Your treasure simply refers to your possessions, resources, and finances. All these are received from God. They are blessings from a loving God to you. Your response must be to honor Him by making these resources and finances available in humble service when God requires them. "Honor the Lord with your wealth and with the best part of everything you produce. Then he will fill your barns with grain, and your vats will overflow with good wine."[24]

There is enough proof that the uncommon armorbearer who serves the Lord is entitled to the best rewards of prosperity, health, success and long life. "So you shall serve the LORD your God, and He will bless your bread and your water. And I will take sickness away from the midst of you. No one shall suffer miscarriage or be barren in your land; I will fulfill the number of your days." [25]

I. God will bless your food and water.

The uncommon armorbearer enjoys the reward of a need-free life. You will have in abundance everything you need for a well-balanced life with nothing missing or broken around you.

II. God will protect you from sickness.

The uncommon armorbearer enjoys the reward of a sickness-free life. You will be strong supernaturally and physically fit so you can keep on discharging your duties in service. A lifestyle of service offers you the best health insurance package and benefits.

III. God will not let you suffer miscarriage.

The uncommon armorbearer enjoys the reward of a sorrow-free life. You will have experiences that will bring you joy only with no regrets. You will be exempt from the tragedies and woes of life.

IV. God will not let you be barren.

The uncommon armorbearer enjoys the reward of a stagnation-free life. You will be productive and enjoy the results of your work. You will enjoy maximum returns for little effort and investments.

V. **G**OD *WILL GIVE YOU A LONG FULFILLED LIFE.*

The uncommon armorbearer enjoys the reward of a long fulfilled life. You will live long while making a difference in the lives of others.

Chapter Seven
ARMORBEARING 106
The Leadership of Servanthood

*"The most important one of you should
be like the least important, and your leader
should be like a servant."*[1]

THE SERVANT LEADER

There is a leadership dimension to a lifestyle of service.
As a true leader, a lifestyle of service sets you apart and
unlocks the flow of greatness and significance in the
kingdom of God. Leadership according to Jesus is not
in status or in position; rather it is in service and disposition. It requires you to act as if you, though the
leader, are the least important and that you become
the one who serves. Therefore, every true leader is a
servant leader.

SERVANT LEADER DEFINED:

#I. **A SERVANT LEADER IS THE ARMORBEARER WHO LEADS THROUGH SERVICE.**

A servant leader serves as an example for others to follow. This is the essence of true servant leadership. It is leading by service; serving God and His agenda on the earth. As a servant leader, you are not about your own agenda but you are about God's agenda. Looking at every great man in the Bible, you will discover that they all launched into their greatness and entered their significance through this principle of servant leadership, through serving God and His cause on the earth, every one of them. Men like Abraham, Isaac, Jacob, Joseph, Moses, David, Nehemiah, and Paul; all excelled and made a difference because their disposition was to lead through service. They all served God and others as servants leading people to their ultimate destination in God's plan and purpose for their lives.

The observable thing that happens to every faithful servant leader is greatness. It is not something that is demanded, rather it is a corresponding manifestation to a lifestyle of armorbearing. When you embrace a faithful life of service, greatness is the reward.

"The one that serves faithfully is the one that enjoys the reward of blessings."[2]

In the New Testament, Jesus tells the tale of the reward of a faithful servant who faithfully executed his task. The faithful servant's master said to him, "Excellent! You've proved yourself not only clever but loyal. You've executed a rather small task masterfully, so now I am going to put you in charge of something larger."[3]

True servant leaders are always in charge! They take the lead by serving. They show others the way to go and render a helping hand along the way. They enjoy helping others succeed and as a testament to their service, they remain pacesetters and role models in their spheres of influence.

#2 A SERVANT LEADER IS THE ARMORBEARER WHO MEETS THE LEGITIMATE NEEDS OF OTHERS.
You are a servant leader when you go about thinking of the best ways to meet the needs of people. It is not about you occupying a position or lobbying for a position, rather it is about you meeting the legitimate

needs of other people. Your highly ranked position does not exempt you from stooping low to render service to those around you.

You can see the premise set by Jesus when He washed the disciples' feet and said, "I am your Lord and Teacher. But I washed your feet. So you also should wash each other's feet. I did this as an example for you. So you should serve each other just as I served you."[4]

Jesus displayed the pattern for servant leadership to His disciples. The Bible records that He took a bowl of water and a towel, and began to wash the feet of His disciples. He found out that these people had a need, and He met the need. Though He is God in human flesh, this job was not beneath Him.

How many people are still like that today that can act like Jesus? He is the "president and founder," yet took a towel and a bowl and washed the feet of His disciples. He did the dirty job to set an example that service is not about the position you occupy, but about the heart you have for people. It is a lifestyle that you must embrace to meet their legitimate needs.

Can you do the "dirty jobs" from your lofty position? Jesus gave the example. He said this is the key to greatness.

#3. A SERVANT LEADER IS THE ARMORBEARER WHO IS A PROBLEM SOLVER.

Problem solving is the art of finding answers to complex questions. It is the process of researching the difficult issues at hand and working through the details until the best solution is reached.

Servant leadership is about being a problem solver. It is about helping others get the answers to their deepest questions and find solutions to their toughest challenges. Being a problem solver is to be like the Son of Man. He did not come to be served. Instead, He came to serve others. "He came to give His life as the price for setting many people free."[5] He became the solution for the problem of sin because sin is everyone's greatest challenge regardless of who they are. Jesus became the Savior of every one who believes in Him. In solving the sin problem, He became the perfect example of a true servant leader. He boldly declared, "The Spirit of the Lord is with me. He has anointed Me to tell the Good News to the poor. He has sent me to announce forgiveness to the prisoners of sin and the restoring of sight to the blind, to forgive those who have been shattered by sin, to announce the year of the Lord's favor."[6]

It is noteworthy that everything Jesus identifies about the purpose of His anointing is channeled toward solving the problems and challenges of people spiritually, physically, socially, and economically.

Unfortunately, we have many celebrities in church today who refuse to stoop low to take the towel and wash the feet of people. They are "so anointed" yet refuse to do anything with the anointing. When asked to take on menial duties, they make remarks like *"Don't you know who I am?"* Then, they run off the list of their accolades, educational accomplishments, and social pedigree, failing to realize that the purpose of the anointing is problem solving.

It is also important to note that using the anointing for problem solving is God's designed way of supplying your needs in the kingdom. God's original design is for your provision to come when you use the anointing on you to solve problems.[7] "Whatever good anyone does, he will receive the same from the Lord."[8]

IT'S YOUR CHOICE

Life is a series of choices you make daily. Becoming a servant leader requires making three vital decisions.

DECISION ONE: BREAK FREE FROM SELF-CENTEREDNESS.

ON JESUS…

HE MADE HIMSELF OF NO REPUTATION, TAKING THE FORM OF A BOND SERVANT, AND COMING IN THE LIKENESS OF MEN.[9]

Jesus freely gave up His rights, privileges, and dignity to assume the role of a servant. Only someone that has broken free from self-centeredness can do that. If you are so conscious about yourself and your status, you cannot do that. Rather, you cling on to your ego, which blinds you to the truth of how out-of-tune you are. When you make comments like, *"Don't you know who I am?" "That kind of work is beneath me," "I can't do that,"* or *"I can't serve there,"* this is pride in manifestation. When in pride, you eliminate God from the equation of your life and downfall is the only end result.[10]

You must break free from self-centeredness. We live in a world today where we are too much into ourselves. This is the reason those with legitimate needs around us are either unnoticed or ignored. Jesus became poor so that through His poverty we can become rich. He was someone who was not all about Himself. He tasted death so we can live the good life.

Jesus chose to break free from self-centeredness. You must make the same choice to become a servant leader, a true armorbearer.

DECISION TWO: TAKE RESPONSIBILITY FOR SACRIFICIAL SERVICE.
MORE ON JESUS...
HE WAS BORN AS A MAN AND BECAME LIKE A SERVANT.[11]

The Holy Trinity had a divine meeting in heaven concerning what to do about the salvation of the human race. The resolution of the issue required divinity to put on humanity. Jesus stepped up to the plate. He said, "This job is not beneath me, I will go to the earth. It is a sacrifice to go but I will do it!" He took ownership of this most important task to save the human race. You see, unless you claim ownership of the task, you will not take the responsibility for the outcome. This has been the missing link. No wonder the bottom of the ladder is so crowded when God wants us to be at the top. Claiming ownership leads to taking responsibility. If you see the assigned task as yours, you generally will not be slack about doing it excellently because you will see the responsibility as yours.

Choose to take responsibility always because a servant is a steward with the mentality of an owner.

DECISION THREE: PUT ON HUMILITY.
LASTLY ON JESUS...
WHEN HE WAS LIVING AS A MAN, HE HUMBLED HIMSELF AND WAS FULLY OBEDIENT TO GOD, EVEN WHEN THAT CAUSED HIS DEATH—DEATH ON A CROSS.[12]

It takes humility to serve. If you have any iota of pride, you cannot be a successful servant leader. Pride is like a disease that eats you up from within just to destroy you.

"Pride goes before destruction and a haughty spirit before a fall."[13] You will never meet him but if you ever did, ask Lucifer. It was pride that pulled him down because he was self-centered; everything was about *"me, mine, and myself."*

The Bible says, "How you are fallen from heaven, O Lucifer, son of the morning! How you are cut down to the ground, you who weakened the nations! For you have said in your heart: 'I will ascend into heaven, I will exalt my throne above the stars of God; I will also sit on the mount of the congregation on the farthest sides of the north; I will ascend above the heights of the clouds, I will be like the Most High.' Yet you shall be brought down to Sheol, to the lowest depths of the Pit."[14]

You must eradicate pride from your life because it hinders you from serving well. It takes humility to serve, and every one that embraces this, experiences promotion and greatness in life.

"Humble yourself in the sight of The Lord and He will lift you up."[15]

Humility is the stuff that the solid character needed for selfless-service is made-up of, and it is the foundation to build a great life on. You must choose to put on humility as a lifestyle.

Chapter Eight

ARMORBEARING 107
The Grace to Serve

Therefore, since we are receiving a kingdom which cannot be shaken, let us have grace, by which we may serve...[1]

THE GRACE TO SERVE

The grace to serve is a divine empowerment that God puts on you, which gives you an unquenchable disposition to service. It is a divine influence given to you by God that allows you to give yourself wholeheartedly, spirit, soul, and body to serving and expressing good-will toward others. Without the grace to serve, it will be quite impossible to perform your responsibility as an armorbearer. "Therefore, since we are receiving a kingdom which cannot be shaken, let us have grace, by which we may serve God acceptably with reverence and godly fear."[2] However, to have this grace you must know and be in your sphere of influence. Your ultimate purpose is to serve since you were created to serve, but to fulfill that goal takes knowing your own personal purpose in life.

"Most assuredly, I say to you, unless a grain of wheat falls into the ground and dies, it remains alone; but if it dies, it produces much grain."[3] The grain of wheat cannot die unless it falls into the ground. It remains one grain and can never become more until it falls *into the ground.* It is the death of the grain that causes it to transform and produce much new grain, but it cannot die unless it falls *into the ground.*

Therefore, until you are *in the ground* of your personal divine purpose, you cannot have the grace to serve as you should. You have to know God's divine purpose as it relates to you personally so you can be empowered with the grace to serve as a true armorbearer.

Many people struggle with dedicating themselves to a lifestyle of service because they are yet to discover their personal divine purpose, but those who have a passion to serve are those that are in God's personal divine purpose for their lives. They are round pegs in round holes, so they are fulfilled personally and focused on the ultimate assignment of armorbearing.

If you are a square peg, your focus will be on fitting in the round hole and, ultimately, you lose sight of the great responsibility of service. Plus, you will end up bruising the square and destroying its structure.

Listen to this, the greatest tragedy is not death but a life without a purpose; that is, being alive and never knowing why. It is like climbing the ladder of success to the top, only to find out it is leaning on the wrong building. Without purpose, your life has no meaning. You will simply live through each day with no bearing whatsoever.

DIVINE PURPOSE PLATFORM

Have you discovered God's personal divine purpose for your life? Do you know why you are here?

You see, your personal divine purpose is the platform that God has given to you to fulfill the mission and assignment of armorbearing. If you attempt to fulfill this mission and assignment on any other platform, it really becomes a struggle and you will be frustrated.

Salt loses its taste, its strength and quality when it is not stored in the right place. For example, if stored in a moist place and water gets into it, then it loses its saltiness and usefulness, and will end up in the garbage can. This end becomes inevitable because the salt was not stored in its divine place of destiny.

"You are the salt of the earth, but if salt has lost its taste, strength, or quality, how can its saltness be restored? It is not good for anything any longer but to be thrown out and trodden underfoot by men."[4]

God told Jeremiah, "Before I formed you in the womb I knew and approved of you as My chosen instrument, and before you were born I separated and set you apart, consecrating you; and I appointed you as a prophet to the nations."[5]

Jeremiah's personal divine purpose, and what God had in mind for him, was to be a prophet to the nations. On that platform, he would carry out the great task of armorbearing. If he had attempted to become anything else, he would have been a frustrated man.

Therefore, your personal divine purpose is the platform for enjoying the grace to serve as a true armorbearer. For you, this is where it must begin. You must be where God wants you to be!

DISCOVER YOUR DIVINE PURPOSE

Your personal divine purpose is hidden within you and you have the responsibility to discover what it is. Here are a few pointers to help you.

#1: ASK GOD.

God said "Ask Me, and I will tell you things that you don't know and can't find out."[6] This is a vital pointer to know your divine purpose, you must go to God in prayer. He said to ask Him and He will tell you about your purpose. He will tell you the problem of humanity He created you to solve and on that platform you become His voice and instrument.

JEREMIAH

In the conversation with God about his divine purpose, Jeremiah said, "Ah, Lord God! Behold, I cannot speak, for I am a youth." God replies, "Do not say, 'I am a youth,' for you shall go to all to whom I send you, and whatever I command you, you shall speak. Do not be afraid of their faces, for I am with you."[7]

When you are in your divine purpose, you will never be afraid of the faces of those you are to serve. You are a solution to somebody! You have the responsibility to discover your divine purpose so that you can be the solution to that person. Somebody needs you. But you must ask God your creator, and He will surely tell you. Not only that, He will release on you the grace to serve on that platform.

The Lord reached out His hand, then He touched Jeremiah's mouth and said, "I am giving you the words to say, and I am sending you **with authority** to speak to the nations for me. You will tell them of doom and destruction, and of rising and rebuilding again."[8] When you ask God, He reveals your purpose and also empowers you for service.

PAUL

Paul was a man handpicked by God to be an uncommon armorbearer for Him. At his conversion, God said to Paul, "Rise and stand on your feet; for I have appeared to you for this purpose, to make you a minister and a witness both of the things which you have seen and of the things which I will yet reveal to you. I will deliver you from the Jewish people, as well as from the Gentiles, to whom I now send you, to open their eyes, in order to turn them from darkness to light, and from the power of satan to God, that they may receive forgiveness of sins and an inheritance among those who are sanctified by faith in Me."[9]

After wasting away his adolescent life, Apostle Paul eventually discovered his divine purpose and it was on that platform he was able to fulfill his role as God's armorbearer to the Gentiles. When you discover your divine purpose and run with it by the empowerment of the grace to serve, you are on the pathway to greatness and significance.

#2: FIND WHAT YOU TRULY LOVE.

What you truly love is a pointer to the gifts and talents

in you that will help you discover your divine purpose. Listen, you are not a biological accident! There is something God has put in you that is special and unique. What you truly love and are passionate about is a pointer to your gifts and talents, which could help uncover your divine purpose.

PETER

Peter truly loved fishing. This passionate love to fish was the pointer to his gift, which was the pointer to his divine purpose—to fish for men!

"Jesus, walking by the Sea of Galilee, saw two brothers, Simon called Peter, and Andrew his brother, casting a net into the sea; for they were fishermen. Then He said to them, 'Follow Me, and I will make you fishers of men.' They immediately left their nets and followed Him."[10]

Peter discovered his divine purpose and received the grace to serve. He became one of the greatest armorbearers that ever lived.

MOSES

Moses truly loved people. He had a passionate love to help and get justice for them. He hated to see injustice and boldly stood against it. "When Moses was forty years old, he wanted to help the Israelites because they were his own people. One day he saw an Egyptian mistreating one of them. So he rescued the man."[11]

Moses's passionate love for people was the pointer to his divine purpose as a deliverer. It was on that platform he later became the greatest armorbearer and leader of the Israelites when he rescued them from over four hundred years of slavery. He had the grace to serve because he was in the center of his personal divine purpose.

So what is it that you truly love? What are you passionate about? Do you love children? Music? Justice? Whatever you are passionate about is a clue and pointer to your personal divine purpose.

When you discover what you really love and care about, you must develop your life around it. God has put something special inside you, and He gives the grace to serve so that whatever you are gifted to do is what you keep doing for the rest of your life.

#3: IDENTIFY WHAT STIRS UP "HOLY ANGER" IN YOU.

Whatever stirs up holy anger in you is also a pointer to your personal divine purpose. What I describe as holy anger is a passionate dislike or hatred that is expressed when confronted with what angers God, which is sin. Holy anger toward racism, homosexuality, abortion, poverty, child abuse and the like is a pointer to something you are created and assigned to correct.

Listen, there are many things wrong in your neck of the woods, in your neighborhood, community, city, state, and nation; however, nothing will change until someone moved with holy anger steps forward and takes charge.

I read a Facebook post once that really drives this point home. The post was addressing the case against abortion.

A guy was challenging God: "If you are a loving and merciful God, why can't you send someone to cure cancer and all the terrible diseases plaguing the human race? God replies, "I did, you aborted them!"[12]

I thank God for everything the advocates against abortion are doing, but that problem needs some believers with holy anger to rise up and link the word of God with the gift of life! The holy anger in them will draw on the grace to serve in standing boldly against the indiscriminate termination of these human lives.

Identify what stirs up holy anger in you. What breaks your heart? What deeply saddens and moves you to tears each time you see or hear about it? Do not ignore it. What breaks your heart matters because it also breaks God's heart. He put it in you for a reason, to help you discover your personal divine purpose. When you give it the right focus, you can serve effectively as a true armorbearer.

NEHEMIAH

Nehemiah was a man gravely saddened and discouraged about the state of things in Jerusalem while exiled in Babylon, approximately 423 B.C. His heart broke when he heard the news about the great distress of the people and the destruction of the city walls. He broke down and cried for many days![13] The heart break became the pointer to his divine purpose and the platform for the salvation of a great number of people. This is what armorbearing is all about.

So I ask again, what makes you cry? What saddens you? What moves you to tears? What breaks your heart? How do you feel about all the wrongful killings, sex trafficking, liquor billboards, drunk-driving accidents, and terrorism? These are pointers to divine purpose and a platform to receive the grace to serve as God's armorbearer.

What is your response going to be?

IN CONCLUSION

The chosen faith I practice teaches that the Bible is the inspired word of God. Everything in Scripture is God's word. All of it is useful for teaching and helping people and for correcting them and showing them how to live. The Scriptures train God's servants to do all kinds of good deeds."[14]

I entered into a covenant with God some years ago because I saw in His word that service is the only way out of the land of poverty, into the land of prosperity. I saw that serving God is the only way out of lack into abundance. You also can make the same commitment today to be in a covenant of service by saying, "Lord, all the days of my life I will serve You and Your agenda in the earth. I come into a covenant with You that all the days of my life, I make Your business as my business and Your agenda as my agenda. So help me God."

When you enter a covenant of service with God, He will do wonders in your life. This has been my experience since I made this covenant thirteen years ago. God said that when I serve Him: "He'll bless *my* food and *my* water; He'll get rid of the sickness *from me*;

134 Armorbearer: A Life of Service

there won't be any miscarriages nor barren women in *my* land. He'll make sure *my family and I* live full and complete lives."[15]

God is always in search of people who have made this covenant of service, so He can lift them into greatness and significance in life. However, it is one thing to make a covenant and another thing to carry out the terms of the covenant. To do that, what you need is the anointing. This is the reason God anointed David with the grace to serve.

God said of David: "I have found My servant David; with My holy oil I have anointed him, with whom My hand shall be established; Also My arm shall strengthen him. The enemy shall not outwit him, nor the son of wickedness afflict him. I will beat down his foes before his face, and plague those who hate him. But My faithfulness and My mercy shall be with him, and in My name his horn shall be exalted."[16]

All these promises are because of the anointing upon a man who made a covenant of service and a commitment to be God's armorbearer.

PRAYER:

Father, in the name of Jesus, anoint me afresh with the grace to serve as Your armorbearer; anoint me that I may serve You with my heart, with my mind, with my strength and with my all. Father, anoint me to be relevant in Your agenda for humanity. Amen.

ON A PERSONAL NOTE

Your source of power is God. His divine grace flows to keep you functioning in life successfully, but a lifestyle of sin stops the flow of God's grace. Until sin is dealt with, you cannot obtain the passport for your great success journey. The good news is that Jesus already paid the penalty for sin. All you have to do is pick up the passport of salvation.

The Bible says, "Believe on the Lord Jesus Christ, and you will be saved, you and your household."[1] Furthermore, "If you confess with your mouth the Lord Jesus and believe in your heart that God has raised Him from the dead, you will be saved."[2] If you believe, acknowledge Jesus as your Savior and Lord, then, you will experience a change in your heart. Say this prayer with me:

Lord Jesus, I confess and ask You to forgive my sins. I believe You died on the cross and rose again just for me. Be my Lord as from today. I surrender my life to You. Thank You for my salvation! In Jesus's name, Amen!

ABOUT THE AUTHOR

Tolu Areola is an insightful teacher, minister, speaker, administrator, and author. His teaching anointing is based on the belief and truth that the word of God works when practiced.

He is a former architect who delivers a fresh and practical insight to the word of God that empowers people to live the life of success and prosperity God planned for them. He is passionate and committed to helping people experience God's best for their lives and fulfill their God-given destinies.

Tolu renders his stewardship under the leadership of Pastor Toye Ademola, the presiding pastor of Dominion International Center Worldwide, for whom he has had the privilege to be associate and armorbearer for two decades. He is currently the administrative director of Christ Tower Ministries International, a dynamic ministry whose mission is to raise kingdom leaders.

He resides in Houston, Texas, with his wife, Tomi, and their two children, Joy and Joshua.

Appendix

Quotations noted **AMP** are from *The Amplified Bible,* copyright ©1954, 1958, 1962, 1964, 1965, 1987 by The Lockman Foundation, La Habra, CA. All rights reserved. Used by permission. www.lockman.org.

Quotations noted **CEB** are from *The Common English Bible,* copyright ©2012, P.O. Box 801 201 Eighth Avenue South Nashville, TN 37202-0801

Quotations noted **CJB** are from *The Complete Jewish Bible* by David H. Stern, copyright ©1998. All rights reserved. Used by permission of Messianic Jewish Publishers, 6120 Day Long Lane, Clarksville, MD 21029. www.messianicjewish.net

Quotations noted **CEV** are from *The Contemporary English Version,* copyright ©1991, 1992, 1995 by American Bible Society. Used by permission.

Quotations noted **ERV** are from *The Easy-To-Read Version,* copyright ©2006 by World Bible Translation Center

Quotations noted **EXB** are from *The Expanded Bible,* copyright ©2011 by Thomas Nelson. Used by permission. All rights reserved.

Quotations noted **GW** are from *God's Word*®, copyright ©1995 God's Word to the Nations. Used by permission of Baker Publishing Group.

Quotations noted **Phillips** are from *J. B. Phillips, "The New Testament in Modern English",* copyright ©1962 edition, published by HarperCollins.

Quotations noted **KJV** are from *The King James Version.*

Quotations noted **TLB** are from *The Living Bible,* copyright ©1971 by Tyndale House Foundation. Used by permission of Tyndale House Publishers Inc., Carol Stream, IL 60188. All rights reserved.

Quotations noted **MSG** are from *The Message,* copyright ©1993, 1994, 1995, 1996, 2000, 2001, 2002. Used by permission of NavPress Publishing Group.

Quotations noted **NCV** are from *The New Century Version*®, copyright ©2005 by Thomas Nelson. Used by permission. All rights reserved.

Quotations noted **NIRV** are from *the New International Reader's Version*®, copyright ©1995, 1996, 1998, 2014 by Biblica, Inc.®. Used by permission. All rights reserved worldwide.

Quotations noted **NIV** are from *The New International Version*®, copyright ©1973, 1978, 1984, 2011 by Biblica, Inc.® Used by permission. All rights reserved worldwide.

Quotations noted **NLT** are from *The New Living Translation,* copyright ©1996, 2004, 2007 by Tyndale House Foundation. Used by permission of Tyndale House Publishers, Inc., Carol Stream, IL 60188. All rights reserved.

Quotations noted **Voice** are from *The Voice*™, copyright ©2008 by Ecclesia Bible Society. Used by permission. All rights reserved.

Quotations noted **WEB** are from *The World English Bible,* Public Domain.

Quotations noted **WE** are from *The Jesus Book—The Bible in Worldwide English,* copyright ©1969, 1971, 1996, 1998 by SOON Educational Publications, Willington, Derby, DE65 6BN, England.

Notes

Introduction

1. Matthew 16:19.
2. ibid.
3. Isaiah 5:13.
4. See Acts 5:34–39.
5. Philippians 2:9 CEV paraphrased.
6. 1 John 4:17.

Chapter One

1. Jeremiah 29:11 CEV.
2. Jeremiah 29:11 CEV paraphrased.
3. Colossians 1:19–22.
4. See http://www.onelook.com/?lang=all&w=servant.
5. James Strong, Strong's Concordance 5375.
6. Strong's Concordance 3627.
7. 1 Samuel 14:6–7 NLT.
8. Luke 4:18–19 NCV.
9. Mark 10:45 NIV.
10. Luke 22:27.
11. See 1 John 4:17.
12. See Genesis 1:26.
13. See Psalms 82:6.
14. See Exodus 8:1; 9:1.
15. See Psalms 139:13–14.
16. Jeremiah 1:5 NCV.
17. See 1 Corinthians 6:20; 7:23 TLB.
18. Ephesians 2:10 NCV paraphrased.
19. 1 Samuel 16:18, 21.
20. Matthew 5:13.
21. See Genesis 1:1–3.
22. Matthew 5:14–16.
23. Matthew 5:14–16 MSG.
24. See John 1:1–5; 3:19–21.

Chapter Two

1. Mark 10:43–44.
2. Mark 10:37 MSG.
3. Mark 10:40.
4. Mark 10:42-43.
5. See Mark 10:43.
6. Proverbs 13:12.
7. Mike Murdock, Wisdom Commentary Volume 2 (The Wisdom Center: 2003), p. 49.
8. ibid., p. 50–51.
9. See Mark 10:46–52.
10. Psalms 37:4.
11. Philippians 2:5 AMP.
12. See http://www.macmillandictionary.com/dictionary/american/humility#humility_3.
13. See Mark 10:42–43.
14. 1 Peter 5:6.
15. See Philippians 2:5–11.
16. Jesus on Leadership, p. 48 by C. Gene Wilkes, ref: Celebration of Discipline by Richard J. Foster.
17. See http://www.merriam-webster.com/dictionary/faithfulness.
18. 1 Corinthians 4:2 paraphrased.
19. See Hebrews 3:5.
20. See Proverbs 28:20.
21. See Nehemiah 9:7–8; Genesis 15:18–21.
22. Matthew 25:14–21 NIV paraphrased.
23. See 2 Timothy 2:1–5.
24. Proverbs 11:3 CEV.
25. Proverbs 10:9.
26. See Luke 2:46 CEV.
27. ibid.
28. Romans 10:17 CEV.
29. Proverbs 9:9.
30. See Hosea 4:6; Isaiah 5:13.
31. See Jeremiah 33:3.

32. James 1:5–8 TLB paraphrased.
33. John 3:16 CEV paraphrased.
34. Deuteronomy 10:12 NLT.
35. 1 Corinthians 13:4–7 paraphrased.
36. See Numbers 14:17–20.
37. See Acts 14:17–20.
38. See http://www.livescience.com/41742-influential-leaders-who-transformed-the-world.html *emphasis mine.*
39. 1 Corinthians 13:8.
40. See Daniel 1:17–20.
41. 1 John 4:18 CJB.

Chapter Three

1. Matthew 16:24 WEB.
2. See John 5:30 paraphrased.
3. Philippians 2:5–8 MSG paraphrased.
4. See John 10:15 MSG.
5. Mark 9:35 TLB.
6. Brian Tracy, No Excuses: The Power of Self Discipline (MJF Books, 2010), p.7.
7. 1 Corinthians 9:24–25 CEB.
8. Mark 10:45 ERV.
9. See Luke 7:1–10.
10. See Genesis 24.
11. See Genesis 39:1–5.

Chapter Four

1. 2 Corinthians 6:17.
2. See Luke 2:49.
3. See John 5:30.
4. Genesis 39:7–9 MSG, emphasis mine.
5. James Hunter, The World's Most Powerful Leadership Principle (WaterBrook Press, 2004), p.109.

6. Dwight Lyman Moody, (February 5, 1837–December 22, 1899), also known as D. L. Moody, was an American evangelist and publisher who founded the Moody Church, Northfield School, and Mount Hermon School in Massachusetts, the Moody Bible Institute, and Moody Publishers.
7. See Matthew 9:35–36.
8. Galatians 6:10.
9. Jonah 4:6.
10. See Mark 14:3–9.
11. See Genesis 2:18.
12. John 16:32.
13. Proverbs 18:24.
14. See Deuteronomy 31:7, 23.
15. See 2 Timothy 2:1.
16. See Luke 2:52.
17. Mark 6:31 NLT.
18. See John 1:11 NLT.
19. See Psalms 118:22.

Chapter Five
1. Colossians 3:22 WE.
2. Revelations 3:15–16.
3. See Matthew 26:14–16, 47–50; 27:1–10.
4. See Esther 3:1–6, 12–13.
5. See Esther 7:1–10.
6. Ephesians 6:5–8 AMP.
7. See Luke 15:11–13 MSG.
8. Proverbs 18:9 KJV.
9. See 1 Kings 19:19–21.
10. See 2 Kings 2:1–14.
11. 1 Samuel 20:4 MSG.
12. 1 Samuel 20:17 MSG.
13. Ruth 1:16–17 MSG.

Chapter Six

1. Revelations 22:12.
2. See 1 Corinthians 3:13–15 Phillips.
3. Jeremiah 17:10 NLT.
4. Job 34:11 NCV.
5. See Hebrews 12:28.
6. See 1 Kings 3:6.
7. 1 Corinthians 9:16–17.
8. Psalms 100:2 GW.
9. Ephesians 6:7 NIV
10. 1 Corinthians 15:10 NLT.
11. 1 Corinthians 4:1–2.
12. See Philippians 2:17 EXB.
13. 1 John 3:16 MSG.
14. Colossians 4:12 MSG.
15. Galatians 6:9 CEV.
16. Psalms 2:11 AMP.
17. Job 34:11.
18. Luke 18:28–30 NLT.
19. Jeremiah 1:7 MSG.
20. See Luke 2:36–37 paraphrased.
21. John 9:4.
22. Proverbs 18:16.
23. See 1 Corinthians 7:7.
24. Proverbs 3:9-10 NLT.
25. Exodus 23:25–26.

Chapter Seven

1. Luke 22:26 CEV.
2. See Proverbs 28:20 paraphrased.
3. See Matthew 25:21 Voice.
4. See John 13:14–15 ERV.
5. Matthew 20:28 NIRV.
6. Luke 4:18–19 GW.

7. See Luke 10:1,4; 22:35.
8. Ephesians 6:8.
9. See Philippians 2:7.
10. See 1 Timothy 3:1–6.
11. See Philippians 2:7 NCV.
12. See Philippians 2:8 NCV.
13. Proverbs 16:18.
14. Isaiah 14:12–15.
15. James 4:10.

Chapter Eight

1. See Hebrews 12:28
2. ibid.
3. John 12:24.
4. Matthew 5:13 AMP paraphrased.
5. Jeremiah 1:4–5 AMP.
6. Jeremiah 33:3 CEV.
7. See Jeremiah 1:6–8
8. See Jeremiah 1:9–10 CEV emphasis mine.
9. See Acts 26:16–18.
10. Matthew 4:18–20.
11. See Acts 7:23–24 CEV.
12. Author unknown, paraphrased.
13. See Nehemiah 1:1–4.
14. 2 Timothy 3:16–17 CEV.
15. See Exodus 23:25–26 MSG paraphrased.
16. Psalms 89:20–24.

On a Personal Note

1. Acts 16:31.
2. Romans 10:9.

AUTHOR CONTACT

Additional copies of this book are available from your local or online bookstore, in e-book format, or contact the following:

Tolu Areola
P.O. Box 721242
Houston, TX 77272
contact@empowermentfortoday.com
www.empowermentfortoday.com
(281)401-9887

www.ingramcontent.com/pod-product-compliance
Lightning Source LLC
Chambersburg PA
CBHW071547040426
42452CB00008B/1104